WHAT PEOPLE ARE SAYING ABOUT

IN10TIONS

With compassion and great love, Melissa's *In10tions* takes you on a journey to a new life by guiding you to replace negative thoughts and behaviors with positive and empowering inner shifts. If you've lost confidence, or given over to pessimism, this book will show you the way home.
Cynthia Occelli, author, Radio Host, and Founder of the Beautiful Life School

This book, along with Melissa, came along in my life at a time when a whirlwind of opportunity was swirling around me. As a therapist and entrepreneur, building a business of holistic healing for highly traumatized individuals, it has been easy to become overwhelmed as the world presents challenges, solutions, and demands. Wanting so much to create a welcoming, effective healing environment for others and to promote the awareness and success of my fellow healers, I found little time for my own centering. *In10tions: A Mindset Reset Guide to Happiness* reminds us that a simple yet profound approach can reset your life. The brain is a most amazing organ and recent research in neuroplasticity shows us that this center of thought can either program us or be programmed by us, allowing us to overcome the hurts and adaptive responses designed to protect our basic selves from real and perceived hurts. Much of my practice is helping people to undo the programming in their life that no longer serves them, holds them back or seems to imprison them in their pain. Traumatic experience brings about a complex brain response naturally designed to protect from current and future threat. There is increasing scientific evidence that effective therapeutic interventions to manage pain, resolve

PTSD and rewrite life stories employ the principles of brain science and neuroplasticity, including NLP. As I read through this guide, I found myself excited for many of the people who come to me – this is a wonderful tool that is easily integrated into daily life and can support as well as guide the therapeutic process. Change takes work and sometimes work in the form of gentle self-care generates compliance and follow through. Simple yet elegant, easy to follow yet quite profound, this guide is a must for the reception area as well as therapy room, as well as the private setting for the healer to recharge and redirect so as to more healthfully continue the vital work that we do.
Vicky Primer, PhD., Certified EMDR Therapist

We have the choice, what will you choose? Is how Melissa leads us into a non-stop happiness transformation guide of 90 powerful affirmations to reset our intentions to unlimited love, abundance and bliss as we were destined to have during our lives on this planet. The choice is ours. Will we live in the darkness or step toward the light? With *In10tions*, we step confidently on the path of recognizing and actualizing our inherent power within. *In10tions* is a gift for every man or woman born on this planet, as we are each miracles, and this book is a manifester of the miracles we already are but somewhere along the way, forgot to be.
Samantha Marie Davis, Founder of Lipstick Affirmations (#lipstickaffirmations)

In10tions is an example of a person's creativity, positivity, and purpose manifesting itself into a book. Melissa has so much to offer from her personal experiences and as an expert in the meditation which she pours into this book. Make meditation a part of your DAILY LIFE now and use this book as your launchpad.
Ritu Ashrafi, Atma Kriya Meditation Teacher and Founder of TheLifester.com

Finally a book that will not only help you change temporarily to the better, but also help you confirm a great new habit! Melissa exudes goodness, and has created a magical guideline that she is sharing with the world. Our mind is our most powerful tool, and with these simple steps, she is helping us open up to the possibilities each and very one of us are capable of. As she states in her book, "Personal development isn't always rainbows and butterflies! But the reward of your personal self-discovery makes all the heartache and challenges well worth it." Who can argue with that? Now if you haven't already, go read the book!
Dimitra Kotanides, Yoga Instructor and Owner of Dimitra Yoga

By providing an overview as to why 90 days is an effective period to devote to one's personal growth – by allowing the brain to reset itself – *In10tions* permits the mindset to redirect its course toward something that often eludes many; inner peace.

Even with a busy lifestyle, with this book and its easily implementable steps, all you need are 10 minutes each day for 90 days and a true commitment to rejuvenate your spirit, revitalize your life, and radiate growth. Things we can all do in a snap!

Whether you are an avid practitioner of meditation or yoga, a fitness enthusiast, or not quite into any of these, *In10tions* is a book that belongs in every hand attached to a mind seeking inner peace and spiritual fulfillment.
Geneva Fonda, professional photographer and writer

In10tions is a book for those seeking a way to focus daily. It provides positive activities for readers to engage in that will enlighten their minds and encourage their spirits. Melissa is a natural with making others feel great and this is evident through the pages of this book!
LaQuisha Hall, Founder of iEAT (Empower. Aspire. Transform) and author of *Positively Bodyful*

In10tions: A Mindset Reset Guide to Happiness is a an easy-to-use, practical guide to meditation. It is also serves as a 90 day make-over manual for a mind in need of transformation. Melissa provides a simple formula for taking control of your state of mind. Take 10 minutes in the morning to meditate on a positive intention. Re-visit the intention throughout the day as life's inevitable challenges arise and take 10 more minutes at night to reflect on how setting the positive intention affected the rest of your day. To make it even easier, she provides the postive intentions in clear, straightforward language. If you've been intending to meditate, or planning to become more positive, or hoping to feel happier this is the book for you. I highly recommend it.

Jan Krause Greene, author of *I Call Myself Earth Girl*

In10tions

A Mindset Reset Guide to Happiness

In10tions

A Mindset Reset Guide to Happiness

Melissa Escaro

Foreword by Joe White

Winchester, UK
Washington, USA

First published by Soul Rocks Books, 2015
Soul Rocks Books is an imprint of John Hunt Publishing Ltd., Laurel House, Station Approach,
Alresford, Hants, SO24 9JH, UK
office1@jhpbooks.net
www.johnhuntpublishing.com
www.soulrocks-books.com

For distributor details and how to order please visit the 'Ordering' section on our website.

Text copyright: Melissa Escaro 2014

ISBN: 978 1 78279 602 2
Library of Congress Control Number: 2014945007

All rights reserved. Except for brief quotations in critical articles or reviews, no part of this book may be reproduced in any manner without prior written permission from the publishers.

The rights of Melissa Escaro as author have been asserted in accordance with the Copyright, Designs and Patents Act 1988.

A CIP catalogue record for this book is available from the British Library.

Design: Stuart Davies
www.stuartdaviesart.com

Printed in the USA by Edwards Brothers Malloy

We operate a distinctive and ethical publishing philosophy in all areas of our business, from our global network of authors to production and worldwide distribution.

To Mom & Dad, whose great intentions created who I am.
Thank you, I am forever grateful and I love you.

Foreword

Change is such a big ambiguous word. There are thousands of titles of books that offer you the opportunity to change. Change your mind. Change your body. Change your relationship. Change your soul. But is change what we really seek? Think about it. You can change your diet but still not achieve your goals. You can change how you think, but still not have the life you want. Change means to make or become different. So by doing something different, that will give us the life that we desire? Maybe, but only if the change we make takes us in the direction we want to go. Let's say you are from the North and you want to go to Texas. You begin your journey only to realize that you are heading west not south, so you change your direction and then you start to travel east. Have you created a change? Yes, but are you any closer to the dreams you want to have? No!

We need something better than "Change" to work with. Something that more accurately describes what we desire and who we are. The very word "Change" presupposes that who you currently are is not good enough and that you will need to change something to get that which you desire. I have always seen that as a bit of painting yourself in the corner, making it more difficult than needed.

I rather look at this as transformation. Transformation is more about taking what you already have and making improvements where needed. It presupposes that all that you need is within you already and that refinement and growth will get you to your destination.

Now the question becomes, how do I get there? Ahhhh, you are in for a treat because you are holding the answers in your hand! Melissa will take you on amazing journey of the daily steps to help you cultivate one of the greatest of all emotional states… Happiness. Melissa hits the nail squarely on the head by using the mechanics of conditioning to help you take some small simple steps that in a short period will grow exponentially until one day soon you will begin to realize how happy you have become. You will be surprised and even amazed to where your level of happiness will be at the end of this book.

For the past twenty-one years, I have been fascinated with *Why do we do what we do?* My first interest came in the form of a lifeboat that saved me from the drowning waters of my addiction to cocaine and alcohol. I overdosed and was brought back from the dead. I was depressed and seeing a psychologist and psychiatrist. Then I discovered some self-help audiotapes and by listening to them began to transform my life. In desperation I became a sponge, soaking up any and all knowledge that I could. I started to realize that my life was a bunch of patterns and within those patterns there are mechanics, principles and laws and that I was not inherently bad or broken, but rather, my mechanics were off. I was running a bunch of old and outdated patterns that did not serve me. I learned that I could change those patterns and unlearn all that did not serve me and learn new patterns that would transform my life. I did just that. I became a sponge, learning more and more about anything that had to do with why we do what we do and how to change those patterns to better, more resourceful patterns.

In 1999, I opened my company, Get Life Coaching, with two coaching clients in the basement of my house. To date I have worked with over fourteen thousand people to transform their emotions, their lives, businesses, bodies, wealth and relationships. So when Melissa asked me to write this foreword for this amazing book, I was deeply honored and excited for you, the recipient of Melissa's gifts. I say that because the foundation of this book is based on the simple but timeless principle of conditioning yourself for the life you want, intermixed with amazing tools and tons of heart from Melissa.

People often underestimate the power of conditioning. They confuse awareness with action. Awareness is the first step of transformation but action is where the rubber meets the road. With action you have knowledge in application.

The key to success begins with the understanding that everything we think say, feel and do is a pattern and that all patterns are learned. How are they learned? There are two major ways that a pattern is learned. One is that we do it over and over again. Repetition. It is like building a muscle. You go to the gym one time, do some curls and a bench press. You feel some soreness in your muscles but you never go back. How much muscle have you built? Not much unless you go back to the gym over and over again. Repetition is the genesis of greatness. Without repetition learning is a long, long road.

The second key is that which gets reinforced will grow and become stronger. The interesting fact is that reinforcement can work for us or against us. Let me explain. A child gets great grades and the parents make a huge fuss over it. They praise the child, give him all significance and love the child desires. Do you think the next time the child has a test will they work as hard or even harder to achieve the good praise? Yes, most of the time, especially if the praise is consistent.

Let's say that same child brings home the good grades, but the parents are too wrapped up in life and the child gets barely a smile. The child feels ignored and that happens over and over. Do you think eventually that child will feel unnoticed? Unrecognized? Perhaps not enough? Yes, and then one day, the child brings home a bad grade and the parents are upset. They make a big fuss about the bad grade. They yell and talk to the child over and over about this situation. What happens in the child's mind? Well, they wanted love and positive attention, but unlike the first example, this child does not get positive reinforcement, so will settle for negative attention, which is better than no attention. Whatever gets reinforced, positively or negatively, will happen again and again, whether it feels good or not. We must learn to use this as a tool of mastery, not a tool of disempowerment.

Learning a new habit or pattern is usually awkward, uncomfortable, frustrating, or challenging. This is not because there is something wrong but rather there is something right that is happening.

There are four levels to conditioning to your identity. The first is Unconscious Incompetence. That means you don't know what you don't know. That is where you are with this book and the valuable tools in these pages. Second is Conscious Incompetence, which is where you now know what you don't know. It is a humbling experience, but a natural process. Awareness is what we must have in order to transform. The third level is Conscious Competence. We can now do the task, but it takes a large amount focus. This is the awkward stage. It seems artificial and unnatural. Many people stop here and that is the biggest shame because this is the moment before your biggest breakthrough yet. If you keep on pushing, keep on focusing on what you want not what you don't want, you will arrive at level four, Unconscious Competence. This is where you do it because it is who you are; it has been conditioned to your identity. Congrats, you have made it!

So I am excited for you, as you are about to begin a magnificent transformation. Remember this key – let it be easy. No need to make it harder on yourself then need be. Enjoy the journey, the hills and valleys and above all honor you by becoming the best you that you can be.

I wish you love and passion and Live Free!!
Joe White
President and Founder of Get Life Coaching
Master Firewalk Instructor

Introduction

"The state of your life is nothing more than a reflection of the state of your mind."
Dr. Wayne W. Dyer

Our intentions are powerful beyond belief. They determine who we are and help us with the manifestation of what we want in our lives. Good or bad, intentions pave the road of our own personal journey, of who we are and who we become. An intention sets the pace of our actions and how we create our desires. An intention set with compassion and love can lead us on a path of service to others, which benefits others, and our own need to feel that what we do matters in this world. An intention set with jealousy or malice creates a result that is one dimensional, fear-based, and filled with low energy. Intentions are the first step in our daily action plans and within them lies great significance that we need to pay attention to. What we think matters, because it reflects how we feel, and the actions that we take.

My mom was the first person who introduced me to the concept of manifestation. "Think positive thoughts and surround yourself with positive people" is her motto. Growing up I was surrounded by affirmations, positivity, and unconditional love, and my enthusiasm for life and self-confidence reflected this. I was the lead in my elementary school's musicals and the girl with the wacky and wild fashion sense in high school. Growing up, I played by my own rules, took risks, and was considered a "free spirit" by my friends. I collected and read books on the power of manifestation, methods to incorporate affirmations into your life, and how to shift towards a positive mindset. I created vision boards, cutting out pictures of beautiful images of places I wanted to visit and things that I wanted in my life. I was fascinated about the study of people, leading me to pursue my degrees in psychology and clinical social work, in an attempt to understand how and why people think the way that they do. I had a thorough logical understanding on how powerful our thoughts could be and knew exactly what needed to be done. I gave this information to friends, following the same advice my mom gave me "Think positive." "Surround yourself with positive people." "Keep it on the positive!" I was the positivity princess among my friends.

But I am human and like everyone else, insecurity and self-doubt got in my way. My level of confidence shifted, going through periods where I felt like I was on top of the world and others where I felt like I didn't have a clue. It's the feeling you get when all the girls in your class stop talking to you for no reason at all or the panic you feel when you are in a lecture hall and have no idea what your professor is talking about. I faced reality where life can be harsh and foster so much negativity, and I wasn't able to tune in to what I knew was true. For a period in my life, the intentions that I set for myself were not serving me in any means. I felt incomplete. I struggled with not feeling good enough, smart enough, thin enough, loveable enough, and deserving enough. The intentions I had set...well they were awful, and focused on all of my inadequacies and shortcomings. I struggled with identifying who I was and what role I should play in this world. I lost sight of my true core self. Many of us have this same struggle, but at the time I thought I was all alone in this. I was the only one with this problem (my level of significance was high!), causing me to isolate myself from others. My intentions created a vicious cycle and a life of low energy. I felt that I had nothing to celebrate, so my life remained stuck in standstill. I was unable to move forward, and in many cases I moved backwards. I did not see that I was the one responsible for creating this negativity in my life.

The peak of my struggle was during my twenties into my

Introduction

thirties, which was a huge transition phase for me. I had lost myself in my twenties, hoping to find myself in my thirties. I struggled with the internal debate of "What do I want to do when I grow up?" This decade is a period of uncertainty for many people, where we are supposed to determine: who do we want to be, what do we want to do, who do we want to do this with, and how are we going to do it? College, career, marriage, money...there is a lot going on during this decade and it is overwhelming. It is a period of soul searching and a recipe for a quarter-life crisis...which is exactly what I felt like was going on in my life. I can certainly attest to making some bad choices during this time. There were plenty of things I did to numb out the uncomfortable feelings of uncertainty, from too many party-filled nights, obsession with my weight and appearance, co-dependence in mediocre relationships, and the need for control of every little thing possible in my life. All these things filled me up artificially, but I didn't feel whole, and I certainly didn't feel like myself.

It wasn't until I started a dedicated meditation practice that I began to really make some shifts in my life. On my thirty-fifth birthday, I made a promise to myself to make yoga a non-negotiable practice in my life... I had been practicing yoga on and off for years prior, but never fully took the leap to make it an integral part of my life. I always liked the way yoga made me feel on and off the mat, not only from a physical standpoint, but a mental and spiritual one as well. I felt more open, grounded, and clear. Why I had never dedicated myself sooner to something that created these desired feelings for me, I don't know; perhaps my internal thoughts of unworthiness told me I wasn't worthy of this time and space for myself.

I was emotionally exhausted and drained. I was tired of the excuses and feeling awful. I was ready for some positive change and my life to truly begin. I had confided to one of my friends that I refused to do anything that didn't make me happy. This was a bold statement and turning point for me. For so long, I chased dreams that weren't mine to begin with. They were things that I thought I should do, but didn't have a place in my heart. So I signed up for a yoga membership, knowing that this was something that I wanted and I was worthy of receiving this gift from myself.

Through yoga, I was able to dive deeper into my meditation practice. As I tuned into my breath and body, being in the present moment, I shifted into a state of just being. It became a little easier each time to get to this place and I have been learning to redirect myself here when my mind begins to wander. After seeing the benefits of decreased anxiety and more emotional openness, I decided that a dedicated meditation practice would be in my best interest. It has been one of the best personal self-care decisions that I have made for myself to date.

One of the reasons I wrote this book was to educate people on how significant inner reflection can be and how to get started. In everyday conversation, I encounter so many people who are amazed that I am dedicated to this time and receive a lot of comments of disbelief that they could do the same. "I don't have time to meditate." "I couldn't sit still for that long." "I would get bored with the silence…" Many people don't get started with meditation because of their fear that it is complicated or they won't do it right, yet it doesn't have to be complicated and anyone can do it. Meditation just takes a little time from your day and an intention to how you want to feel.

There are a ton of different philosophies on how to meditate and a lot of resources to help someone get started. I am a believer of making this practice simple, so that it becomes another routine to your day. The first thing I did was create a meditation station, an area where I would practice that was away from any distractions. It is the one space in my home that I know I can go to and feel completely at ease.

When you first start a meditation practice, you aren't quite sure what to do. "So you just close your eyes and just sit there?" one of my friends asked me when I started to explain how to build a meditation practice. Well, yes, essentially you do, and with time you learn how to shift inward and allow whatever sensations you experience to come up. Trust that your unconscious mind knows what you need in that moment. The key to remember is there is no one "correct" way to meditate, you do what works for you.

I began my practice with a word or a phrase to keep me grounded. Every day is different. Some words that I have utilized have been "love", "faith", and "surrender". These words set an intention for my practice, what I want to focus on, and invite it to enter into my life. I found my focus words to be extremely helpful, not only to set the tone for my meditation practice, but to put me into a state that induces the emotions of these words. These intentions guided my practice, gave me clarity, and helped ground myself when my mind was racing. Throughout my practice, I would come back to my intention and allow my mind to settle. I wanted to share how intention setting helped me build a meditation practice and this is how *In10tions* was born.

The Mechanics of Conditioning In10tions to your Identity

When I first started using intentions, I did so because they felt good. They were positive, uplifting, and shifted my perspective to one that was more open. It wasn't until I started exploring neurolinguistic programing as part of my life-coaching education that I realized what I was doing was conditioning these beliefs to who I was. In fact, when you explore this process, you discover it actually is quite mechanical, despite the free-flowing nature of meditation and inner reflection.

Neurolinguistic programing (NLP) is an approach to communication and personal development that was created by Richard

Bandler and John Grinder in the 1970s. It focuses on connecting neurological processes within the brain, language patterns, and behavioral patterns through experience. As I explored NLP, I made the connection that the intentions I was setting and the methodology behind them was a form of conditioning. The intentions that I set though writing them down, reading them, thinking about them, and saying aloud began to not just become something that I did, but a part of who I was. The more often I practiced intention setting, the easier it became, and soon it was ingrained as a part of me. My intentions became a daily part of my life by writing them in the morning, saying them out loud in the shower, repeating them while walking my dog, or surrounding myself with them on Post-its throughout the house and in my car.

As you explore your own intention setting, you will create a similar experience. With time, it will become natural to have a morning and evening routine to take you inward. But remember, any new habit we will do when it is easy and convenient; doing it when it is hard is the key to success. There will be days you will not feel like reading your in10tion or writing in your journal. I have experienced this multiple times throughout my life, going through "droughts" of personal development. The key to making lasting change is making the change a part of your identity. Conditioning this change requires repetition, which is why this book is written with two daily activities for ninety days. The uniqueness of inward meditation, reflection, and journaling, along with the emotional intensity of owning the in10tion as a part of who you are will condition these new positive beliefs to your very core and your true authentic self.

How to use this book

I created *In10tions* for individuals who want to experience meditation, but don't know how to start. In10tions takes impactful focus words and creates a comprehensive and wonderful intentional incantation that has a focus you can breathe in, feel, and experience. They are simple and to the point with honesty that people can appreciate. Meditation shouldn't be intimidating. Sure, I love mudras, chanting, and the traditions of meditation but not everybody does or feels a little out of place when they first start their practice. In10tions is a simple tool that you can use to build your practice, whether you are new to meditation or have been meditating for some time. This book is designed to help you create a reflective state wherever you are and align your identity with the true nature of your core.

In10tions are for individuals who are on a journey of self-discovery. All of us have experienced some tough times, have limiting beliefs, or have made some poor choices and are feeling beaten down, unhappy, and worst of all, unworthy. Each in10tion that is written in this book explores ways you can let go of old negative thought beliefs and welcome a new set of affirming, positive, and loving thoughts. Simply put, *In10tions* replaces your negative thoughts with positive ones.

In10tions is a ninety-day mindset reset. Why ninety days? Ninety days is usually when most employee benefits begin, when many return policies end at retail stores, and the completion of a woman's first trimester. It is also the basis of many rehab programs... AA usually requires new members to attend one meeting a day for the first ninety days. It has been stated that ninety days is the amount of time needed for the brain to reset and release the influence of a drug. It takes forty days to change a habit; it takes ninety days to confirm that habit, incorporating it into who you really are. My hope is that you will use this book as a tool to reset your mind and shift towards a more positive way of thinking. As you change your mindset to one that is more positive, affirming, and happy, the world around you shifts towards one that is more positive, affirming, and happy. You can create the life that you want and deserve with the power of your intentions. This book serves as a guide for you to do just that, by retraining and re-wiring your brain.

So what does the 10 mean in In10tions? 10 represents ten minutes of your day that you will be resetting your mindset. Traditional meditation can go on for much longer, even hours at a time, but if you are the average person, balancing work, family and other obligations you may not have this luxury (you barely have time to read this book!) or you may not have yet committed more time to your practice. When I first started my meditation practice I was gung ho. I was going to have an amazing, transcendental, and enlightening experience! I was going to meditate for an extended period of time and it was going to be beautiful. Well, it turns out, that every day doesn't allow us to have these ideal situations. Rather than beat myself up for not spending a massive amount of time with self-reflection, I wanted to set myself up to win with a smaller amount of concentrated meditation, which is just as powerful. Ten minutes is a great starting point and an ideal amount of time to reset your mindset. With the consistency of the ninety days, this combination will allow your mind to open up towards more positive beliefs that become a part of who you really are.

In10tions is a two-part process, that may seem so simple, but the results can be so significant by putting in the work and well, your intention. What do you want out of life, what do you want to create and how do you want to feel? Put all of these desires into your intention. Go into your heart, breathe it in, feel who you truly are, and with intention, put this into your practice, so that the results will reflect in your everyday life.

Each day will begin by reading an in10tion to set the tone for your day and begin the process of resetting your mindset. Sit comfortably in your meditation station and read the day's message first silently, then aloud with intensity. Feel the words that you say within your heart and own the in10tion as part of who you are. Set your timer for ten minutes, close your eyes, and allow it to settle in. You may have urges during this time to fidget or think about doing other things. This is not the time to plan your grocery list! If the silence is unbearable, take the focus word from the in10tion and repeat it silently in your mind. Take this time for you to allow the in10tion for the day to resonate within you in whatever shape or form it may come to you. You may experience something, or you may experience nothing. Trust your unconscious mind that you are exactly where you need to be. Just know that taking ten minutes at the beginning of your day is a fantastic starting point for the reset of your mind and to set the tone of your day.

At the end of your day, revisit your in10tion. This is a time for self-reflection, to see if you were able to practice this in10tion. Every day is going to be different; some days you may be able to rock this new mindset and others you may struggle and run your old, limiting, and undesirable patterns. Each day is a practice, so don't be so hard on yourself if you are having a challenging day. Give yourself permission to be imperfect and forgive yourself if those outdated beliefs of guilt, unworthiness, and self-doubt slip into the forefront of your mind. It is through the challenges and struggles we encounter that we truly begin to grow. Unfortunately, personal development isn't rainbows and butterflies! But the reward of your personal self-discovery makes all the heartache and challenges well worth it.

The conclusion of your day is a ten-minute journaling session. You may be thinking: "That sounds like a lot of work," or "I am not a very good writer." Journaling has become something that I have learned to appreciate. It reminds me of that diary that many of us used to have, the one with a lock and key built in where we wrote all of our secrets with truth and vulnerability. Like anything else, journaling takes practice and consistency to see the benefits. You can't train for a marathon in one day; you must start off with small intervals and build your way up. This is the same with journaling.

At the end of every in10tion is a set of three evening reflection questions. These questions explore how you interpreted the day's in10tion, utilized it that day, and how it will impact you in the future. Read the questions, reflect on your day, and write from your heart. Remember, this is your experience and there are no wrong answers, so write freely. Write for the full ten minutes without stopping and just allow the mind to let go. Write whatever comes to your mind, even if it doesn't make sense. It is at that point when the most astounding and insightful thoughts can appear. I love the power and impact journaling can have on a person, because it gives you an opportunity to put your thoughts to paper. To think of an idea is one thing, but when you place it visually on paper for the eyes to see and interpret, that is a powerful tool, especially with conditioning these new beliefs to your identity. Some of the greatest breakthroughs I have personally experienced have been when I have openly written what my fears and hopes are, and what needs to happen in my life, openly, freely, and truthfully on paper.

I suggest you get a journal that is visually appealing to you, something that you would love to see every day. It is the same concept as creating your space for your meditation, to surround yourself with calming and uplifting things so that you can experience the moment on all visceral levels, from what you see, hear, and feel. Take the full ten minutes of journaling and use it to put all your thoughts to paper. There is no formal format; you could answer the questions in order, write your answers in story form, or you could even just use the questions as a guide and free write. The experience is yours; do what feels best for you.

So there you have it, your in10tions plan. Ten minutes of meditation in the morning, focusing on an intentional thought and ten minutes of journal reflection of how you brought that thought to action that day. Ninety days of practice leading to a transformation towards your authentic and true self.

Introduction

My Hope for You

My hope for you is that this book will be a beginning step towards your transformation. I believe that we are all powerful beings, and have more power that we give ourselves credit for. We have the ability to change our life, for better or worse, within an instant...just with the power of our thoughts. The quality of our life is our choice. We can choose to think small, to live a life of suffering, which we induce upon ourselves. We can choose to work the job that we absolutely loathe day in and day out, feeling frustrated that we are not contributing or growing to our greatest capacity. We can choose the relationship that is unfulfilling or toxic because we are afraid of change or are uncertain of what the future will hold if we open ourselves up. We can choose to hold back our deepest thoughts and feelings of vulnerability and not love fully with an open heart. We can choose the thoughts that we are undeserving, unloveable, and we are not enough. Or we can choose to think higher thoughts focused on love; mind-boggling love for that matter! We can live a life that is abundant, vibrant, and beyond our wildest dreams. We can be in a career where we love what we do and are rewarded both financially and spiritually. We can live our purpose, giving and loving to others through courage and faith with and open heart. We can have relationships of pure happiness, not based on jealousy or conditional love. We can choose thoughts that we are love, we are abundant, and we are enough. We have the ability to create our own reality, filled with love, purpose, and passion. We have the choice, what will you choose?

Today is a brand new day. Let your intentions ignite and excite you as you start your journey of passion for life and self-discovery!

Day 1:
I let go of anger to make room for good

In10tion Focus: Good

Today's in10tion focuses on letting go of all of my angry thoughts. Anger towards a person or about a past situation does not serve me in a positive way. My anger masks my underlying feelings of fear, which keep me from moving forward and allowing good to enter my heart. As I meditate today, with each breath out, I let go of all angry and resentful thoughts and with each breath in, I allow good intentions to enter my heart.

Evening In10tion Reflection

1. In what areas in my life have I been holding onto anger?
2. How has this anger translated to my body, mind, and spirit?
3. How would I like to feel instead?

The heaviest chains that hold us back can be released through the power of good intentions.

Day 2:
If I think it, I become it

In10tion Focus: Visualize

Today's in10tion focuses on my goals and aspirations. Visualization is a powerful tool that can be used to manifest my dreams. The more that I believe in something and believe in myself, the better the chance to create the opportunity to make things happen. As I visualize my dreams in today's meditation, I utilize all of my senses to create a real experience. With each breath, I live the visualization in my mind and repeat "If I think it, I become it."

Evening In10tion Reflection

1. What would I like to become?
2. How can I change my thoughts to manifest this creation?
3. What steps can I take to strengthen my inner beliefs so that I can create positive change?

Possibilities become reality with the shift of a thought.

Day 3:

No worries today

In10tion Focus: Carefree

Today's in10tion focuses on letting go of all of my day's worries. Daily challenges cause me to worry about things. Today I won't worry, as these troublesome thoughts do not serve me in a positive manner. I replace my worries with the calming affirmation "No worries today." In today's meditation, I breathe in calmness and I breathe out all of my worried thoughts that weigh down my heart.

☽

Evening In10tion Reflection

1. What am I truly worried about?
2. What kinds of feelings do I want to have instead of anxiety?
3. What other affirmations can I use to ease my worries?

Release all the worries, challenges, and stress that sit heavy in your body. lightening and brightening your heart.

Day 4:

Be kind to others and kindness will find me

In10tion Focus: Kind

Today's in10tion focuses on treating others with the same kindness that I want to receive. Kindness is as simple as a smile or an out-of-the-ordinary gesture, both which warm the heart. Kindness creates kindness and as I radiate this, it will find me in return. I remind myself that kindness is unlimited and I can give and receive without limits. As I breathe today, I open my heart to giving and receiving unlimited kindness.

Evening In10tion Reflection

1. In what ways can I express kindness?
2. How would I like to receive kindness?
3. How can I stay on a path of unlimited kindness?

Kindness can be a simple touch, nod, or smile, all with the intention of compassion behind it.

Day 5:

Live, love, sparkle

In10tion Focus: Sparkle

Today's in10tion focuses on living my life fully, loving every minute of it, shining my light, and sparkling towards everything and everyone. Life is a blessing and I enjoy every moment. I am bright, sparkle and shine and nothing can dim my brightness. I realize that as I continue to be vibrant, life will become better and brighter. In today's meditation, I envision a bright sparkly light surrounding me, reminding me to go forth in life wholeheartedly and love all those around me.

☽

Evening In10tion Reflection

1. How can I live a life that sparkles and shines?
2. What things in my life dull my sparkle?
3. What will my life be like when I am able to live vibrantly?

Our inner light compares with the night sky of sparkling stars shining upon the world.

Day 6:

I will get through this

In10tion Focus: Perseverance

Today's in10tion assures me that no matter what may be happening in my life; that I will get through it. I am a strong individual and have all the tools and skills within me to endure whatever hardships may come my way. I believe that things will work out for me and will not let my fear take over. I believe in the highest good and that I am taken care of. In today's meditation, I focus on all of my internal strengths and faith that there is a plan for me.

Evening In10tion Reflection

1. What am I afraid of at this time?
2. What strengths do I have to help me through this struggle?
3. How will faith serve me at this time?

Courage and faith are the foundational pieces of inner strength.

Day 7:

I live today like a vacation

In10tion Focus: Light

Today's in10tion focuses on living my day like a vacation: carefree, hopeful, and happy. I look at each day with this perspective, bringing a lighthearted inner peace forward. I look forward to the wonderful experiences that I will have today. In today's meditation, I focus on feeling light with each breath in and let go of heaviness with each breath out.

☽

Evening In10tion Reflection

1. What does my ideal vacation look and feel like?
2. How can I take aspects from my ideal vacation and apply it every day?
3. What can I do now to lighten my day?

Imagine your magical escape within, knowing that you have the power to return here at any time.

Day 8:

Tomorrow really is another day

In10tion Focus: Gentle

Today's in10tion is a reminder that I will continue my journey tomorrow. I am gentle with myself if I don't get everything accomplished today. Tomorrow really is another day, so I live today fully. In today's meditation, I celebrate all the accomplishments I have made today and look forward to what I will achieve tomorrow.

☽

Evening In10tion Reflection

1. What is something that happened today that I am proud of?
2. In what areas do I need to be more gentle with myself?
3. What am I looking forward to tomorrow?

Dream of the next chapter of your story, turning the page from today to a fresh page tomorrow.

Day 9:

Today I ask for a miracle and am ready for its arrival

In10tion Focus: Miracle

Today's in10tion focuses on my belief in everyday miracles and allowing miracles to come my way. Miracles occur every day around me and remind me that I am worthy of them. I believe in miracles and surrendering myself to this belief allows them to enter my life. In today's meditation, I focus on the existence of miracles, I ask for one, and I open myself up to its arrival.

Evening In10tion Reflection

1. What are the miracles that I believe in?
2. How can I open myself up to miracles appearing in my life?
3. Why am I worthy of a miracle?

Miracles happen for those who believe in them and are willing to wait, without knowing when they will arrive.

Day 10:

True love is unconditional

In10tion Focus: Love

Today's in10tion focuses on unconditional love to all those in my life. Often times the ones closest to me are the ones who hurt me. Although it may be unintentional, it still hurts. I love the individuals I am close to unconditionally and with each breath focus my love onto them. In today's meditation, I focus on unconditional love and kindness and let go of any anger and resentment.

Evening In10tion Reflection

1. What hurt am I willing to let go and forgive?
2. How can I love unconditionally?
3. How can I focus my unconditional love onto others?

To love unconditionally without expectations is not only courageous, but exemplifies true compassion.

Day 11:

When opportunity knocks, I run to the door

In10tion Focus: Opportunity

Today's in10tion focuses on acting on opportunities that are presented to me. An opportunity is not a coincidence; there is a divine plan for me. I act with urgency when an opportunity comes my way and won't let it slip by. In today's meditation, I become more aware of the opportunities that are presenting themselves to me and focus my energy on seizing them.

☽

Evening In10tion Reflection

1. What opportunities are knocking at my door?
2. How can I act upon opportunities that are presenting themselves to me?
3. What is the divine plan for me?

Life happens for us, not to us, and there are absolutely no coincidences.

Day 12:

The challenge is only in my mind

In10tion Focus: Believe

Today's in10tion focuses on opening my mind's beliefs. I can achieve anything I put my mind to. If I believe something will be challenging, it will be, and if I believe I can accomplish something, I will. The challenge is only in my mind. In today's meditation, I let go of any limiting thoughts and challenges and I bring in positive thoughts of accomplishment.

Evening In10tion Reflection

1. In what areas in my life have I been thinking small?
2. What are my dreams and desires?
3. How will I shift my perception to one that is more positive?

Focus is key to changing the direction to where you want to go.

Day 13:

I treat those around me with the respect that I would want, even through times of doubt

In10tion Focus: Respect

Today's in10tion focuses on kindness and respect to all of those around me. My many choices lead me to feel undecided at times. Despite any of my doubts, I treat everyone with the respect that I would want. In today's meditation, I focus on taking moments of my day to show respect and kindness towards others.

☽

Evening In10tion Reflection

1. How will I show respect and kindness towards others?
2. How do I want be shown respect and kindness?
3. What can I do to make respect and kindness a priority in my life?

Honor your authentic core through actions of respect and kindness to others.

Day 14:
I live my life in person, not virtually

In10tion Focus: Presence

Today's in10tion focuses on living my life in person, not through technology. Because of the vast amount of information, it is easy to get wrapped up living a virtual life. I live my life by creating relationships and appreciating wonders that are happening around me. In today's meditation, I focus on living my life in the present though connection.

Evening In10tion Reflection

1. How has social media and technology played a role in my life?
2. How can I live my life more in person?
3. How can I balance my virtual and in-person life?

Through connection and creating relationships, we nurture the art of conversation.

Day 15:

I am perfect as is

In10tion Focus: Imperfect

Today's in10tion focuses on how wonderful and perfect I am in this moment. I embrace who I am and living authentically makes me perfect. I love myself for who I am. In today's meditation, with each breath in, I bring in feelings of self-love, and with each breath out, I release any feelings of self-loathing.

☽

Evening In10tion Reflection

1. How do I define myself?
2. What things do I love about myself?
3. What self-loathing feelings am I ready to let go?

The celebration of how perfectly imperfect we are is truly liberating!

Day 16:
My "New Year's" resolutions start now

In10tion Focus: Dream

Today's in10tion focuses on starting on my "New Year's" resolutions today! I will not wait for "the right time" because the right time is now. I move forward towards my goals with a positive attitude, knowing that I can achieve what I set my mind to. In today's meditation, I focus on bringing my resolutions to the present moment and start my work towards them today.

☽

Evening In10tion Reflection

1. What resolutions and goals am I looking to achieve?
2. What has been holding me back from pursuing these resolutions?
3. How can I start working on my resolutions today?

We have the ability to make all our dreams come true by stepping forward now.

Day 17:

Leadership begins with me

In10tion Focus: Leader

Today's in10tion focuses on being a leader in all areas of my life. I am a vehicle for positive change and lead others towards positive change by making the first step. I initiate positivity and inspiration for others. In today's meditation, I focus on being a leader, making the first step towards positive change, and creating a difference.

☽

Evening In10tion Reflection

1. What qualities make a good leader?
2. How am I a good leader?
3. How will my leadership impact those around me?

As you step forward into the unknown, remind yourself that leaders go first.

Day 18:

I choose to be happy

In10tion Focus: Happy

Today's in10tion focuses on my choice of happiness. I choose to embrace a positive outlook and invite happiness in. I surround myself with people that bring me joy. I am present in my happiness. In today's meditation, I focus on choosing happiness, knowing that I have the ability to bring happiness into my life by embracing it.

Evening In10tion Reflection

1. What things make me happy?
2. What feelings have I been choosing instead of happiness?
3. How will I invite happiness into my life?

Every action that we make and thought that we have is a choice, and influences the potential of happiness that we can have in our life.

Day 19:

I am mindful of the critic inside of me

In10tion Focus: Acceptance

Today's in10tion focuses on mindfulness of my self-criticism. I am aware of times that I am being hard on myself and examine my underlying feelings. I replace all feelings of criticism with love and accept and love myself for the person that I am. In today's meditation, I focus on being mindful of the critic inside of me, recognizing when I am being critical, and let go of all negative thoughts, focusing only on the positive.

☽

Evening In10tion Reflection

1. In what areas of my life have I been critical of myself?
2. How will I replace criticism with love?
3. What positive thoughts about myself will I shift towards?

Rather than being our own worst critic, why not be our biggest fan?

Day 20:

I must love myself first

In10tion Focus: Authentic

Today's in10tion focuses on loving myself first so I can give this love to all others. I am reminded that self-love is the best gift I could give myself, which enables me to contribute towards others. I love myself for the beautiful individual that I am on the inside and out. With today's in10tion, I radiate with self-love, focusing on all the beautiful and unique characteristics about myself.

☽

Evening In10tion Reflection

1. What makes me beautiful and unique?
2. How can I love myself more each day?
3. What will my life look like when I truly love myself?

True beauty lies within our core, through our authenticity, graciousness, kindness, and love.

Day 21:

I believe in the good in me and other people

In10tion Focus: Optimistic

Today's in10tion focuses on seeing all the good in myself and other people. I believe that we are all working together towards living a peaceful and loving life. I am a vessel for good and I have a lot of love and compassion to give. I believe that we are all working together towards a common good. With today's in10tion, I look at the good in all individuals and myself.

Evening In10tion Reflection

1. What are the good things I see in myself?
2. How can I see the best in other people?
3. What are the good things that I have to give to others?

Rather than focus on all that is wrong in this world, through gratitude we can shift our perspective to all that is right.

Day 22:
Changes begin in me

In10tion Focus: Change

Today's in10tion focuses on changes that I make within myself, which creates change in my community, and within the world. I am a leader of change and capable of making a better life for myself and others. I am not afraid of change and embrace it as part of my learning journey. With today's in10tion, I welcome change into my life with an open mind and open heart.

☽

Evening In10tion Reflection

1. What changes am I looking forward to making?
2. What changes am I afraid to make?
3. How will I overcome my fear of change and welcome it into my life?

As we move through change, recognizing the discomfort of uncertainty is merely a signal of growth.

Day 23:
Clean my body, clear my mind

In10tion Focus: Health

Today's in10tion focuses on cleaning my body on a physical level to clear my mind and open myself to more possibilities. I treat my body as a physical vehicle for my growth. I treat by body with love and respect and fuel it with vibrancy and energy. With today's in10tion, I associate a clean body with a clear and open mind.

☽

Evening In10tion Reflection

1. How do I treat my body now?
2. How can I treat my body with more love and respect?
3. What kind of possibilities will appear to me by cleaning my body?

Our bodies are temples to be kept clean, clear, and magnificently decorated.

Day 24:

My life is abundant and full

In10tion Focus: Abundance

Today's in10tion focuses on all the abundance and fullness that already resides in my life. I do not need to look outside for abundance, because I already have all that I need. I remember that my life is full and I am very blessed to have so much fortune in my life. With today's in10tion, I celebrate all that is already in my life, allowing more abundance to come my way.

☽

Evening In10tion Reflection

1. What kind of abundance do I have in my life?
2. What are the blessings I am thankful for?
3. How can I remind myself of all the abundance and blessings that are in my life?

As we express gratitude for all that we have, all that we need will present itself to us.

Day 25:

There is no such thing as bad days

In10tion Focus: Experience

Today's in10tion focuses on the good in each day, even the most challenging days that cause us despair. Darkness exists so that light can shine. Even if the day seems bleak, today I am awake and alive, so it is a good day! With today's in10tion, I look at each day as magnificent and an opportunity for beautiful things to be created.

☽

Evening In10tion Reflection

1. What kind of good did I experience today?
2. How can I see the good in each day?
3. How can I shine bright through a dark day?

Today is a good day, tomorrow is a great day, and the future is open to unlimited possibilities.

Day 26:

I remove "I can't" from my vocabulary

In10tion Focus: Unstoppable

Today's in10tion focuses on my ability to accomplish anything I set my mind to. "I can't" has been removed from my vocabulary and I do not live by this limiting belief. Negative thoughts do not guide my life. I am capable and can do anything! With today's in10tion, I realize that I can, I will, and I am whatever my heart desires!

Evening In10tion Reflection

1. What things in my life have I been telling myself that I can't do?
2. What will my life be like when I realize I can?
3. How will I remove "I can't" from my vocabulary?

When we make our dreams a must, we can do anything.

Day 27:

I appreciate the beauty in all people

In10tion Focus: Beauty

Today's in10tion focuses on seeing the beauty in all people. Every individual has an endearing, beautiful quality, even if it is challenging to see at times. I send positive thoughts to those individuals whose inner beauty may not always shine through, so that they can live as their most authentic self. With today's in10tion, I see beauty and love in every individual.

☽

Evening In10tion Reflection

1. What does inner beauty look like?
2. Where will I look to see inner beauty in other people?
3. How will I see inner beauty in everyone I meet?

By looking into the eyes of others as a reflection of who we are, we understand that we are really one.

Day 28:

A small step is really a huge accomplishment

In10tion Focus: Journey

Today's in10tion focuses on all the small steps that I am taking towards my never-ending improvement and growth. I recognize that change is challenging and sometimes painful, and acknowledge that all of my small steps are huge accomplishments that create big changes. With today's in10tion, I acknowledge all the significant steps I have taken and will continue to take on my journey.

Evening In10tion Reflection

1. What small steps have I already taken on my journey of life?
2. What small steps am I looking forward to taking now and into the future?
3. How will my small steps build to bigger things?

The joy of the journey is the steps that we take towards our destination.

Day 29:

When in doubt, breathe it out

In10tion Focus: Breath

Today's in10tion focuses on using my breath to help me through moments of doubt. As I face challenges, I use my breath to help me re-focus, calm my fears, and ease my self-doubt. With today's in10tion, I utilize my breath to guide me through any challenge that I may face.

☽

Evening In10tion Reflection

1. In what areas of my life have I been holding my breath?
2. How will I use my breath when I am facing challenges?
3. How will breathing through challenges release my doubts?

Breath brings life, renews the spirit, and enlightens the soul.

Day 30:

Fear exists only if I let it

In10tion Focus: Fearless

Today's in10tion acknowledges that I have a choice to allow my fears to exist. My fears rise from my voice of doubt from within. I look at my fears straight on and consciously choose love instead. With today's in10tion, I let go of fears and choose to not allow them to exist.

☽

Evening In10tion Reflection

1. What fears do I allow to exist?
2. How will I release fears from my life?
3. How will living a fearless life feel?

When faith is stronger than fear, we can live our greatest dreams.

Day 31:

I can only be me

In10tion Focus: Unique

Today's in10tion celebrates the #1 person in my life…me! I am a unique, special, and extraordinary person and celebrate who I am. I am true to myself and this truth radiates to all those around me. I love myself for who I am. With today's in10tion, I reflect on all the goodness that makes up me.

☽

Evening In10tion Reflection

1. What qualities make me special and extraordinary?
2. In what areas of my life have I been holding back who I truly am?
3. How can I express my truth each and every day?

True beauty lies within our authentic core and the more we live true to this, the more we can give back to the world.

Day 32:

Words are a weapon or a tool and I use them with care

In10tion Focus: Empower

Today's in10tion focuses on the words that I use with others and myself. I choose words that reflect positivity, hope, and faith; not discouragement, self-loathing, or hurt. I understand how words are powerful and go deep within our core. With today's in10tion, I am mindful of how I communicate and what words I use to create an uplifting and powerful experience.

Evening In10tion Reflection

1. What discouraging words will I replace?
2. What encouraging words will I focus on using every day?
3. How can I create a positive and uplifting experience for myself and others through my words every day?

Push away the garbage words that drown you and utilize empowering words to raise you up to where you really belong.

Day 33:

I expect good things to happen

In10tion Focus: Knowing

Today's in10tion is my expectation that good things will happen and beautiful things are coming my way. I open my mind and my heart to all the blessings that are coming my way. It is an undeniable knowing that all in my life is well. With today's in10tion, I live my day knowing and expecting goodness, blessings, and love coming my way.

☽

Evening In10tion Reflection

1. What good things are coming into my life?
2. How can I reassure myself that blessings are coming my way?
3. What am I looking forward to tomorrow?

Expect the very best and that is exactly what you will receive.

Day 34:

Today I am still, quiet, and present

In10tion Focus: Reflection

Today's in10tion focuses on quiet reflection, allowing me to receive messages from within. Quieting my mind opens me up to infinite possibilities. I give myself permission to be still and surrender my thoughts. With today's in10tion I am open to stillness, quiet and peace, and listen to what comes to me through this reflection.

☽

Evening In10tion Reflection

1. How will self-reflection open myself up to possibilities?
2. What can I do to create a quiet, meditative state?
3. How will I allow myself to completely surrender?

We cannot hear words of inspiration and possibility until we open up a space of stillness for them to appear.

Day 35:

There is always a reason to celebrate

In10tion Focus: Celebration

Today's in10tion looks at all the reasons in my life to celebrate. Even on my most challenging days, there is a reason to celebrate, whether it is the beauty in nature around me, the beauty within the human spirit, or the fact it is a new day and I am alive. I celebrate all the "little" things in life and realize that they are really "big" things. With today's in10tion, I look at life as a celebration and a reason for joy and happiness.

☾

Evening In10tion Reflection

1. What do I have to celebrate today?
2. What are all the "little things" that I appreciate?
3. How can I be reminded of life's celebrations every day?

Even the smallest accomplishments call for big celebrations.

Day 36:

I view my challenges as opportunities

In10tion Focus: Growth

Today's in10tion views my challenges as opportunities for growth and positive change. I am not discouraged when faced with problems; I do not become overwhelmed by challenges. Instead, I am grateful for the opportunity to grow and learn from the experience. With today's in10tion, I see problems differently, and know that I handle any challenges that I encounter with an open mind and an open heart.

Evening In10tion Reflection

1. How do I view problems and challenges now?
2. How will I shift my perception to see that problems are opportunities?
3. How can I approach challenges with an open mind and heart?

Growth is not for the faint of heart; if you are uncomfortable, celebrate, you are on your way!

Day 37:

I accept compliments with grace

In10tion Focus: Grace

Today's in10tion focuses on receiving compliments gracefully and owning the meaning behind them. I am proud of being recognized for all of my positive attributes and I receive recognition with great pleasure. With today's in10tion I own all compliments that are given to me, accept them as truth, and realize that I deserve them.

Evening In10tion Reflection

1. What compliments have I been given but have not received?
2. What compliments am I proud to be given?
3. How can I accept compliments with grace?

A well-deserved compliment accepted graciously is a beautiful gift to the giver.

Day 38:

Gratitude grounds me

In10tion Focus: Gratitude

Today's in10tion focuses on how gratitude grounds and allows me to live as my true self. I am more appreciative of all the blessings of my life through gratitude. Gratitude helps me "root down" to what is important in my life. With today's in10tion, I appreciate how gratitude grounds me to the reality of all the joy and blessings that are in my life.

Evening In10tion Reflection

1. What am I grateful for today?
2. What is really important in my life?
3. How will allowing gratitude to ground me ignite my true self?

We cannot live in a state of scarcity when we welcome gratitude into our life, inviting abundance in.

Day 39:

I surrender and am ready to let go

In10tion Focus: Surrender

Today's in10tion allows me to surrender. I let go of all thoughts of fear, disappointment, anger, criticism, and guilt. I understand that these thoughts do not serve me. I am ready to let go and move on to positivity, greatness, and love. I surrender and am ready for this. With today's in10tion, I surrender all the negativity that does not serve me and resolve that I am ready to let go.

☽

Evening In10tion Reflection

1. What things in my life am I willing to surrender?
2. What negativity am I looking to replace with greatness and love?
3. How will letting go allow positivity enter my life?

Surrender is not giving up; it is making an empowering decision to mindfully and lovingly release what is no longer serving you in your life.

Day 40:

I endure and survive through the odds

In10tion Focus: Determination

Today's in10tion focuses on my ability to endure and survive. I will encounter tough times where I will want to give up. I will not give up because I am a fighter and can do anything I set my mind to. I have inner strength which guides me to achieve what I set my mind to. With today's in10tion, I trust my determination, inner strength, and drive to accomplish my goals and dreams.

Evening In10tion Reflection

1. What am I willing to endure?
2. What inner strengths do I possess?
3. How can my inner strengths and drive help me achieve my dreams?

Enduring through the challenge is part of the soul's process and integral to the journey.

Day 41:

I am destined for greatness

In10tion Focus: Greatness

Today's in10tion focuses on my belief that I can and will accomplish great things. I am living my life's purpose by following my heart, and by helping others through love, I fulfill my destiny for greatness. With today's in10tion, I have faith that by staying on my path and being true to myself, I will accomplish great things.

☽

Evening In10tion Reflection

1. What great things have I already accomplished?
2. What is my life's purpose?
3. How am I on a journey of accomplishing greatness?

Life is too short for mediocrity, live extraordinarily.

Day 42:

I can handle anything through faith

In10tion Focus: Faith

Today's in10tion focuses on faith and knowing that everything will be ok in the end. I am a strong individual, and through faith I face the darkest of times and the challenges ahead. I handle stress, heartache, and negativity with grace. With today's in10tion, I go to my core belief that despite what may be happening around me, I will get through it.

Evening In10tion Reflection

1. How have I been using faith to help me through challenging times?
2. How will I find faith within to help me through hard times?
3. How will I handle stress and negativity with grace?

Let faith be your co-pilot on your flight through life.

Day 43:

My words of affirmation and positivity create the experiences of my life

In10tion Focus: Positive

Today's in10tion focuses on the use of positive, affirming, and uplifting words to create mirroring experiences in my life. I understand how powerful words are and choose to surround myself with positive ones that will help me through my process. With today's in10tion, I choose positive words to create a positive life experience.

Evening In10tion Reflection

1. What words have I been surrounding myself with?
2. How can I shift my words to ones that are more positive and affirming?
3. What positive words will I use to create a positive life experience?

The language we use directs the soul to the destination that we seek.

Day 44:

I trust things will work themselves out

In10tion Focus: Patience

Today's in10tion focuses on my belief that things will naturally work themselves out for the best. I trust the process that I need to go through and see challenges as opportunities. I embrace patience and allow the process to take as much time as is needed. With today's in10tion, I have faith that I am on the right path and trust the process and journey life takes me on.

Evening In10tion Reflection

1. How will I trust the process that I am going through right now?
2. How can I have a more patient attitude?
3. What can I do to adopt more faith in my life?

Our intuition, which we often underutilize, is a key component to our success.

Day 45:

Today is what matters

In10tion Focus: Today

Today's in10tion focuses on this day and living in the present moment. I am blessed and will make today the very best, full of love, kindness, laughter, and joy. When tomorrow comes, today will be gone and I will leave a legacy of goodness behind. With today's in10tion, I focus on what I can do in this moment to make a positive difference today.

☽

Evening In10tion Reflection

1. How have I lived in the moment today?
2. What am I appreciative of at this moment?
3. How can I make a positive difference in this world today?

Today is yesterday's tomorrow; it is time to start now.

Day 46:

I surrender resistance of being who I truly am

In10tion Focus: Proud

Today's in10tion allows me to embrace my true self and surrender resistance of being who I truly am. I let go of any fears, embarrassment, or shame that I have of revealing who I am to others and stand proud, strong, and with authenticity. By standing in my truth, I open to infinite possibilities and unlimited happiness. With today's in10tion, I surrender my false self and step forward as my true self.

Evening In10tion Reflection

1. How has my false self served me?
2. Who am I truly?
3. What am I open to receiving as my true self?

The greatest gift that we can give to someone is being our true, authentic self, with all of our quirks and imperfections.

Day 47:

Today I take a moment to just be

In10tion Focus: Quiet

Today's in10tion focuses on stillness and being present. I release racing thoughts, to-do lists, and plans and allow myself to be in the moment. Today I relish in quiet, still, reflective moments. With today's in10tion, I find time to just be, live, and breathe in those quiet reflective moments.

☽

Evening In10tion Reflection

1. How can I bring stillness into my life every day?
2. What quiet moments am I looking forward to?
3. How will stillness allow me to reflect?

Quiet reflection inward empowers our dreams outward.

Day 48:

I focus on the beauty of nature to inspire me

In10tion Focus: Nature

Today's in10tion takes me outside into nature to inspire me. I open my eyes to the beauty of nature that I take for granted. I look at each tree, plant and rock with appreciation for its creation and turn to the simplicity of nature for inspiration to live a beautiful and abundant life. With today's in10tion, I see the beauty of nature all around me and use this as inspiration for my amazing day ahead.

☽

Evening In10tion Reflection

1. What nature around me can I appreciate today?
2. How can I incorporate more nature into my life?
3. How will the beauty of nature inspire me today?

The simplicity of nature holds complexity of beauty.

Day 49:

My positive actions heal others

In10tion Focus: Contribution

Today's in10tion reminds me that the positive actions I take help in the healing process of others. My contributions, no matter how big or small, create a higher vibration of energy that others notice and feel. By helping myself first, I become an inspiration of positivity for others. With today's in10tion, I find comfort that my journey is the beginning in a chain of helping others.

☾

Evening In10tion Reflection

1. What contributions have I been making in this world?
2. How am I an inspiration for others?
3. How can I help others on their journey of positivity?

The first step to heal others is to heal ourselves.

Day 50:

I find tranquility in my everyday life

In10tion Focus: Tranquility

Today's in10tion reminds me to see peace and tranquility in simple things every day. I no longer look at mundane activities as boring, but as moments of reflection and contemplation. Meditation is always available to me in my everyday life. With today's in10tion, I shift my perspective to appreciate everyday moments as opportunities for inner change.

Evening In10tion Reflection

1. What mundane activities can become my meditation?
2. In what simple things can I seek peace and tranquility?
3. How will I shift my perception to appreciate the ordinary?

Every movement and every moment is an opportunity for meditation.

Day 51:

I allow love to lead me on my journey

In10tion Focus: Possibility

Today's in10tion takes me on a journey of an open heart through love, rather than the darkness of fear. A journey led through love allows more opportunities for beauty, joy, and miracles. A journey of love creates vulnerability, but the possibilities available through this path are worth the challenges. With today's in10tion, I lead with love on my journey and leave fear behind.

☽

Evening In10tion Reflection

1. How have I let fear lead me on my life's journey?
2. How can I allow love to lead the way?
3. How will taking a journey of love shift and change my life?

We can live our wildest dreams through unconditional and radical love.

Day 52:

My affirming thoughts create my reality

In10tion Focus: Affirm

Today's in10tion reminds me to not let negative self-talk or thoughts sabotage me from the happiness that I deserve. I replace negative thoughts with positive affirming statements. I will not allow the negativity that stems from fear to control my life. I am reminded that I create my reality through my thoughts. With today's in10tion, I focus on positive thoughts and feelings to help lead me towards the life I deserve.

Evening In10tion Reflection

1. What negative thoughts have I been holding on to?
2. How have I gotten in my own way of living a happy life?
3. What positive thoughts will I invite into my life?

Focusing on the affirming moments in our life is a catalyst for positive creation.

Day 53:

I participate in my life

In10tion Focus: Participate

Today's in10tion invites me to live my life to the fullest as a participant. I will no longer sit on the side and watch my life, but live it fully and vibrantly. I enjoy the day fully and linger in each magnificent moment. With today's in10tion, I create a life full of possibilities through activity.

Evening In10tion Reflection

1. Where have I been an observer in my life?
2. How can I participate more in my life?
3. What activities will create a higher vibration for me?

We all have the choice to be the hero in our story.

Day 54:

I am connected with the present

In10tion Focus: Connected

Today's in10tion reminds me to look at this day, this moment, this minute. I stay in the present and let go of insecurities of the past and worries about the future. I am connected with the present through appreciation of the places and people I encounter today. With today's in10tion, I connect with the present, silencing all doubts and fears of the past and future.

Evening In10tion Reflection

1. How am I feeling right now at this moment?
2. What insecurities can I let go now?
3. How can I connect more with the present moment?

Presence is how we connect to the divine within others and ourselves.

Day 55:

I embrace my true, radiant self

In10tion Focus: Embrace

Today's in10tion reminds me to stay on my path of truth and not detour into fear. I remind myself that my feelings of inadequacy and uncertainty are not my true radiant, positive, and beautiful self. I break my patterns of going off course, through gentle affirmations of love and appreciation of myself. With today's in10tion, I focus on thoughts that embrace my true self, staying off a path of self-destruction and fear.

Evening In10tion Reflection

1. How has fear played a role in my life?
2. What gentle reminders of love can I give myself today?
3. How will I stay on my path of truth?

Love and an unbreakable spirit is what keeps us on our path of truth.

Day 56:
I have everything I need today

In10tion Focus: Enough

Today's in10tion focuses on all the blessings and abundance that I have. I remind myself that although I may feel lack, I have everything that I need today. Abundance is part of my life and I notice all the things that I have, including the blessings of my senses to see beauty; the wisdom to make impactful choices; and the amazing individuals who play a positive role in my life. With today's in10tion, I realize that I indeed have it all.

Evening In10tion Reflection

1. What are all the wonderful things I have in my life?
2. How have my feelings of lack affected me?
3. How can I better recognize all the abundance in my life?

Internal satisfaction of who we really are contributes to the magnificent abundance that we have in our lives.

Day 57:
I practice forgiveness starting with myself

In10tion Focus: Forgive

Today's in10tion is a lesson of forgiveness...for myself. I release past poor decisions and stop replaying the negative stories that I have created. By truly forgiving myself, I am able to move forward with love and opportunity for positive change. I am now gentle with myself. With today's in10tion, I allow forgiveness to enter my heart, let go of past hurt and regret, and open up space in my life for love and acceptance.

Evening In10tion Reflection

1. What stories have I created for myself that have not served me?
2. What am I willing to forgive myself for?
3. How will forgiveness open up space in my heart?

The test of forgiveness is to truly surrender to what we cannot control and accept the things we can.

Day 58:

I send love to others that I want for myself

In10tion Focus: Encouragement

Today's in10tion is a lesson in love for those who are struggling and need extra encouragement. I am not different from anyone else, and even though our circumstances may be different, we all share a commonality of needing to feel love. I send love to others as I want and need for myself, and by doing so, create a ripple effect of love on a much larger scale. With today's in10tion, I send caring and positive feelings to all those that I encounter, with a magnitude of love that I would want for myself.

Evening In10tion Reflection

1. Who can I send love to today?
2. How do I want to feel and how can I share these same feelings with others?
3. How are we all connected?

The energy that surrounds us is reflected by the energy we send out to the world.

Day 59:

I remember that we are all more alike than we think

In10tion Focus: One

Today's in10tion reminds me that we are one, and are more alike than we think. Although we have walked different paths in our lives, we share the commonality of a path seeking love, truth, positivity, and a need to feel whole. I embrace the likeness that I have with individuals who may be very different from me. With today's in10tion, I see how alike we are to one another, creating a special bond to those around, allowing me to never feel alone.

☽

Evening In10tion Reflection

1. How have I been separating myself from others?
2. How can I create connections with people who are different from me?
3. How can my awareness of oneness help me on my journey?

Truth is when we can look into the eyes of another and see the reflection of our self.

Day 60:

I trust all my abilities

In10tion Focus: Capable

Today's in10tion challenges me to trust all my qualities, talents, and abilities. I am capable of doing many great things that positively affect others, and trust that I can lead the way with my abilities. I release all self-doubt and insecurities and focus on my good qualities. With today's in10tion, I trust myself, my abilities, and all of my potential.

Evening In10tion Reflection

1. In what areas of my life have I lost trust in myself?
2. What are the things that I trust I am capable of?
3. How can I learn to trust myself more?

Before we can learn to trust other people, we must first learn how to trust ourselves.

Day 61:

I will never give up on my dreams

In10tion Focus: Aspire

Today's in10tion reminds me to follow my heart and never give up on my dreams. There will be times that I get sidetracked, thinking that I cannot accomplish my dreams. I must not forget that I can achieve whatever I set my mind to and that I should never ever give up. I believe in myself and deserve to live my dreams. With today's in10tion, I focus on my aspirations and what I need to do to achieve them, despite any odds I may face.

Evening In10tion Reflection

1. Where have I been sidetracked on my dream journey?
2. What are the dreams that my heart is calling me to?
3. How can I focus more on following my dreams?

Dream big, vivid and bright, for your dreams are the blueprint of the life you desire.

Day 62:

I live an extraordinary life

In10tion Focus: Extraordinary

Today's in10tion proclaims my extraordinary, fantastic life! My life is joyous, unique and full of love, excitement, and variety. I live an extraordinary life! With today's in10tion, I relish in the amazing times in my life, knowing that my experiences are unique, memorable, and fantastic!

Evening In10tion Reflection

1. Where have I been missing the wonders in my life?
2. What is extraordinary in my life?
3. How can I celebrate the fantastic and unique experiences in my life?

Don't settle for the ordinary, strive for the extraordinary.

Day 63:

I look at each day as a learning experience

In10tion Focus: Learn

Today's in10tion reminds me to see the world as my classroom and this day as the lesson. Each experience, joyful or challenging, is guiding me towards my purpose and the lessons that I learn are beautiful and valuable. This world is one large classroom and I am grateful for all of the life lessons that I am learning and experiencing. With today's in10tion, I focus on the value of each lesson I learn and see it as part of my personal growth and lifelong journey.

Evening In10tion Reflection

1. Where have I been missing the lessons in my life?
2. What have been the lessons that I learned today?
3. How can I look at each experience as a lesson?

We must remember that the journey is the lesson.

Day 64:

I believe in my potential

In10tion Focus: Potential

Today's in10tion focuses on believing in myself and all of my potential. I live my very best life, with strong determination and passion. I have the potential to be the person I desire and accomplish the things I set my mind to, when it is true to who I am. With today's in10tion, I tune into my belief that all the potential I need is within me and I have the opportunity to share it with the world.

Evening In10tion Reflection

1. Who do I believe that I am?
2. How can I tune into my inner belief of all of my potential?
3. How can I live my very best life?

Fortune is found when we recognize that the greatest gifts we can give come from within ourselves.

Day 65:

I am passionate with everything I do

In10tion Focus: Passionate

Today's in10tion focuses on giving life my all and putting passion into everything I do. I approach my life with enthusiasm and positivity, and have courage and faith in what I do. When I do something, I act with my entire heart and soul. With today's in10tion, I approach my life full force, and go all in with an enthusiastic, excited, and passionate attitude.

☾

Evening In10tion Reflection

1. How have I been holding back in life?
2. How will I live with an all-in attitude?
3. How will my enthusiasm translate to a fantastic life?

The only thing you can truly control in life is to give it your very best.

Day 66:

It is not what I can get, but what I can give

In10tion Focus: Give

Today's in10tion reminds me that giving is what matters. Giving to others opens my heart, benefits the receiver, and paves a road for future abundance and joy to enter my life. When I give, space opens in my heart, allowing miracles to arrive with the grace intended for them. With today's in10tion, I give to others and create a cycle of receiving positivity and abundance in my life.

Evening In10tion Reflection

1. What have I given today?
2. How can I give more to others?
3. How will my gifts translate into abundance?

To become truly abundant we must give others all of our mind, heart, and soul.

Day 67:

Living my purpose is what life is about

In10tion Focus: Purpose

Today's in10tion reminds me to live my purpose. My ultimate life's purpose is happiness, so I do things that make my heart sing! I make my happiness a priority by taking time to do things that nurture my body, mind, and soul. With today's in10tion, I focus on my purpose in life, living it with joy and an abundance of happiness.

☽

Evening In10tion Reflection

1. What are some things that make my heart sing?
2. How can I nurture myself more?
3. How can I make happiness a priority?

Happiness is singing loudly, dancing wildly, and laughing freely.

Day 68:

Compassion allows my inner beauty to shine

In10tion Focus: Compassion

Today's in10tion focuses on kindness and doing good for others. A small gesture, which may seem insignificant at the time, can mean so much to someone. My true inner beauty shines through more and more when I exhibit compassion to others. With today's in10tion, I allow my inner beauty to shine bright with the simplicity of compassion.

☽

Evening In10tion Reflection

1. Who have I shown compassion to today?
2. How have I been compassionate today?
3. What can I do to express more compassion every day?

Inner beauty of kindness and compassion outlasts all external wonders.

Day 69:

I am amazingly fulfilled

In10tion Focus: Amazing

Today's in10tion celebrates my amazing, beautiful, abundant, and fulfilling life. I am love and I am loved. I have so much goodness in my life and so much to give. I look at each day as a blessing, gift, and opportunity. With today's in10tion, I appreciate my life and its amazing nature.

☽

Evening In10tion Reflection

1. How is my life amazing?
2. What is good in my life right now?
3. How can I celebrate my amazing life every day?

Stop, breathe, and look around at just how utterly amazing your life is.

Day 70:

I believe the highest good is coming forward

In10tion Focus: Blessed

Today's in10tion is a leap of faith that something wonderful is coming my way. I live my day in great optimism, ready to receive great blessings. I let go of anxiety and negativity and look at the good in all things today. With today's in10tion, I have faith that nothing but good is coming forward.

Evening In10tion Reflection

1. What am I looking forward to today?
2. What am I doing to release anxiety and negativity to allow good to appear?
3. How can I rely on faith that blessings are coming my way?

Surrender your fears and realize that the best is yet to come.

Day 71:

I let go of control of things I cannot control

In10tion Focus: Relax

Today's in10tion reminds me to let go of control and let the process lead the way. I remind myself to not be forceful and that I am exactly where I need to be today. The more I relax, the more I am able to feel and allow energy to flow freely in my life. With today's in10tion, I let go completely.

Evening In10tion Reflection

1. How can I let go completely of things I cannot control?
2. How can I relax more?
3. What am I able to let go today?

Let go of what was and what will be, open your heart and fly free.

Day 72:

I do my best to my ability

In10tion Focus: Best

Today's in10tion reminds me to live in this moment and do what I can in this moment. I only can do my very best now, and live where I am. Wherever I go is where I am. With today's in10tion, I celebrate where I am in this moment and remind myself that if I do my best, miraculous things will naturally occur.

Evening In10tion Reflection

1. How am I doing my very best today?
2. What can I do to be in the moment?
3. How can I celebrate the present moments?

Appreciate the beautiful moments now before they become distant moments later.

Day 73:

I sing loudly and dance wildly in life

In10tion Focus: Vibrant

Today's in10tion gives me permission to get a little crazy! I sing loudly, dance wildly, and celebrate my life with enthusiasm and vigor. I am vibrant, juicy, fully engaged, and open to life's possibilities. With today's in10tion, I live my life on a high frequency and vibration.

☽

Evening In10tion Reflection

1. How can I celebrate my life loudly?
2. What makes my life vibrant and colorful?
3. How can I raise my vibration each day?

Enthusiasm, joy and laughter allow opportunity to appear effortlessly.

Day 74:

I expect joy and happiness every day

In10tion Focus: Joy

Today's in10tion is my expectation of joy and happiness each and every day. By expecting this as a normal part of my life, my attitude shifts to one that is more joyful and happy. I know that my life is fantastic! With today's in10tion, I shift my perspective to one that is more positive with a simple expectation of joy and happiness.

Evening In10tion Reflection

1. What are my expectations of joy and happiness?
2. What can I do to create expectations of happiness?
3. How will my expectations shift my perception towards one that is more joyful and happy?

Our thoughts are the masters of our destiny; whether we choose scarcity or abundance is our choice.

Day 75:

What I think, I create

In10tion Focus: Create

Today's in10tion harnesses the power of my thoughts as a vehicle for creation. My thoughts are the beginning of a creative process for the manifestation of my dreams and aspirations. My thoughts are a powerhouse for creation, so I mindfully keep them uplifting and positive. With today's in10tion, I focus on powerful positive thinking as a method of manifestation for wonderful things.

☽

Evening In10tion Reflection

1. What have my thoughts been manifesting?
2. How have my thoughts been driving the direction of my life?
3. How can I create more positive and uplifting thoughts in my life?

Our thoughts are the paintbrush to the canvas of our life.

Day 76:

I give to make my heart happy

In10tion Focus: Open

Today's in10tion practices giving to help others and open up the flow of abundance, happiness, and energy into my life. I give with my words and thoughts, to open up my heart and have my soul sing. When I give to others I receive, opening myself to infinite possibilities. With today's in10tion, I focus on thoughtful giving as a part of my personal power.

Evening In10tion Reflection

1. How can I give to create more abundance?
2. What makes my heart happy?
3. How can I make thoughtful giving an active part of my life?

Giving with an open heart contributes to our growth as vehicles for change.

Day 77:

I embrace the power within me

In10tion Focus: Power

Today's in10tion allows me to own, live, and treasure my personal power. I embrace my power, recognizing my strength and the impact I have on this earth. I have the power within me to create a life that contributes and fulfills. With today's in10tion, I embrace my power with confidence, letting go of insecurities and owning who I truly am.

☽

Evening In10tion Reflection

1. What is my personal power?
2. How can I own who I truly am?
3. What can I do to embrace my power within?

Do not fear the power that is within you, for it is what will begin your awakening and change the world.

Day 78:

I am a unique individual with unlimited potential

In10tion Focus: Limitless

Today's in10tion recognizes my individuality, uniqueness, and internal qualities and talents. I have unlimited potential to create the life that I want and deserve, while touching people with kindness and compassion along the way. With today's in10tion, I recognize that there is a light within me and my purpose is to share it by shining my individuality to the world.

Evening In10tion Reflection

1. How have I dimmed my light and not recognized my uniqueness?
2. What special talents and gifts can I share with others?
3. How will my individuality and uniqueness impact those around me?

The greatest act of selflessness is to share with the world who we really are.

Day 79:

I am gentle and kind to myself

In10tion Focus: Self-love

Today's in10tion reminds me to be gentle and kind to myself. I treat myself with the same dignity and respect as I do others. I release of criticism and harsh inner dialogue and replace these words with positive affirmations of self-love, confidence and respect. It is safe for me to be who I am. With today's in10tion, I welcome kindness into my life, giving myself permission to be who I am.

☾

Evening In10tion Reflection

1. What harsh words have I been telling myself?
2. What kind affirmations can I welcome into my life?
3. How can I feel safe by being who I truly am?

Before we can practice compassion and forgiveness with others, we first must practice this with ourselves.

Day 80:

I replace my excuses with determination and persistence

In10tion Focus: Persistence

Today's in10tion is about action. Excuses are fears that do not serve me, so I let them go and welcome persistence and determination instead. I am a strong and accomplished individual, with infinite potential. I am open to the possibilities that I manifest. With today's in10tion, I recognize that my excuses equate with my fears and as I release them, I allow persistence to lead me to my destination.

☽

Evening In10tion Reflection

1. What excuses have I been using to block me from what I want?
2. How can I invite persistence and determination into my life?
3. What am I looking forward to creating once I let go of my fears?

To get what we want in our life, we must clear space for it to arrive.

Day 81:

I am open to abundance coming my way

In10tion Focus: Appreciation

Today's in10tion opens me to all the abundance coming my way. As I appreciate all that I already have in my life, gates open for more opportunities to enter my life. I have so much to be grateful for. With today's in10tion, I expect abundance and through gratitude, create this in my life.

Evening In10tion Reflection

1. What abundance am I appreciative of right now?
2. How can I open myself up to abundance entering my life?
3. How will gratitude help me become more abundant?

We cannot live in scarcity by adopting an attitude of gratitude.

Day 82:

I find stillness in the busiest of times

In10tion Focus: Stillness

Today's in10tion reminds me to find stillness during the busy and crazy times. I find peace and tranquility within myself, even among the chaos. I quiet my mind and calm my surroundings mindfully through my own means. With today's in10tion, as I still my mind, I create a quiet contemplative environment around me.

☾

Evening In10tion Reflection

1. In what busy times in my life can I find stillness?
2. How can I find stillness in every moment?
3. What can I do to create a quiet environment around me at all times?

When you invite stillness in, astounding things are created.

Day 83:

I welcome change as opportunity

In10tion Focus: Shift

Today's in10tion shifts my perception of change towards a mindset of opportunity. Change creates a shift in my energy as I embrace life with a positive mindset. I embrace change and let go of fear, opening doors for more opportunities to reach me. With today's in10tion, I perceive change joyfully, without apprehension, knowing that change creates a shift.

Evening In10tion Reflection

1. How do I approach change in my life?
2. How can I shift my fearful perceptions to ones that are more open?
3. What will my life by like when I welcome change as opportunity?

An open mind of possibility is a great indicator that change is coming.

Day 84:

I have many choices and options in my life

In10tion Focus: Choice

Today's in10tion focuses on awareness of the choices I have. Despite the odds and challenges that I face, there are always options, even in the bleakest of times. I choose to lead my life with love, purpose, and in my highest good. With today's in10tion, I remind myself that I always have a choice and I choose love and compassion to lead me.

☽

Evening In10tion Reflection

1. When in my life have I believed I had no choices?
2. What are my options during difficult times?
3. How can I choose love during challenging times?

Remember in times of adversity that there is always another move.

Day 85:

I view every person with an open heart

In10tion Focus: Equal

Today's in10tion focuses on looking at every individual with compassion and equality. I open my heart to others and send them my love. I let go of any criticism or judgment and replace them with love. My encounters with people are positive and the energy I radiate has a ripple effect of raising the energy around me. With today's in10tion, I view the world and the people in it with love, compassion, and an optimistic open heart.

Evening In10tion Reflection

1. How can I let go of criticism and judgment of others?
2. How can I look at every individual with compassion and love?
3. How will my positive interactions with others create a ripple effect of love?

Looking for the good in every person cultivates the compassion that may hide from your heart.

Day 86:

I look inward for guidance, not outward to other people

In10tion Focus: Intuition

Today's in10tion encourages me to listen to my inner voice for guidance. All of the answers that I need lie within my mind and soul. I trust my judgment and the actions I take on my journey. I honor myself by quieting my mind and listening to what my inner voice has to say to me. With today's in10tion, I turn inward for guidance, knowing that I trust myself for the answers that bring joy and fulfillment into my life.

Evening In10tion Reflection

1. In what areas have I not trusted my inner guidance?
2. How can I trust my intuition more?
3. How will this trust help me with my personal journey?

Sometimes the quietest voice inside your mind has the loudest impact on your soul.

Day 87:

I am a vehicle for change

In10tion Focus: Impact

Today's in10tion reminds me that I am powerful, energetic, and have the ability to create positive change around me. The choices I make are important, worthy, and make a difference in this world. I am a powerful vehicle for change. With today's in10tion, I am reminded of how much I am needed to make a huge uplifting impact in the world.

Evening In10tion Reflection

1. How am I a vehicle for change?
2. How does the world need me?
3. What kind of impact can I make on this world and the people in it?

The power that lies within us is more powerful than the fearfulness that resides around us.

Day 88:

I love myself and will not shortchange my worth

In10tion Focus: Worthy

Today's in10tion gives me permission to brag about how awesome I am. I love myself fully for who I am and what I stand for. I lead an authentic life, proud of being a compassionate and joyful person. With today's in10tion, I celebrate and love myself fully without shortchanging my worth, because I am priceless.

Evening In10tion Reflection

1. What is important to me and what do I stand for?
2. What do I love about myself?
3. How can I love myself fully and completely?

When you begin to value your worth, you raise the energy around you to draw people and things you need to support your success.

Day 89:

I release all pain and hurt from the past

In10tion Focus: Release

Today's in10tion focuses on my will to let go of pain that I have experienced in my past. The experiences that have hurt me weigh heavy in my body and heart. I embrace a lighter attitude, by forgiving and releasing this weight. I feel light and free and have the ability within me to harness this feeling, despite my painful experiences. With today's in10tion, I release past experiences that burden me and allow myself to float freely towards a new beginning.

☽

Evening In10tion Reflection

1. What pain and hurt has been weighing me down?
2. How can I release this weight and become more light and free?
3. How will releasing my past help me on my journey towards a new beginning?

Each day gives us a new opportunity to love, forgive, and become free from our past.

Day 90:
As seasons change, so do I

In10tion Focus: Emerge

Today's in10tion gives me the ability to view change as a natural part of life. I am constantly changing, as well as the world and people around me. Although the unknown can be frightening, I take comfort knowing that this is only one season in my life and that a new season will be emerging soon. All these changes created the person I am, full of love and contribution to the world. With today's in10tion, I view change as essential and constantly flowing, and I move with this flow without resistance.

Evening In10tion Reflection

1. When have I been resistant to change?
2. What season and changes am I entering into?
3. How will this change help with my transformation?

Be mindful that the stagnant winters in our life will eventually emerge into the growth of spring.

Final Blessing

Congratulations, you did it! How do you feel after completing your ninety-day mindset reset through In10tions? I invite you to reflect how this process has shifted your perspectives and created positive change in your life. Take some time to note the large and small shifts that have happened over the past ninety days, as each change plays an integral role of who you are now in this moment.

So now what? The next day is up to you. Will you conclude this book by returning to your old outdated patterns? Or is this a new beginning for you, perhaps a new chapter in your life? A life full of unlimited possibilities, happiness, gratitude, and love. Maybe this is just the beginning of a new journey to discover who you are at your very core. Have you rediscovered the authentic you who was there all along, hiding underneath all of your fears? Perhaps it is time for you to write your own in10tions, keeping them sacred to your heart. Above all, invite in10tions that will create what you want in your life, while being true to who you really are. I wish you so much love, courage, and faith as you now begin this new journey in your life. Today is just the beginning.

Acknowledgements

There are many individuals that I would like to thank who have contributed to the evolution of this book. I am thankful and grateful for your input, encouragement, and support.

To Melissa Schulte and Samantha Davis, thank you for all of your constructive input and encouragement during the birth of In10tions. Your enthusiasm for the work and its potential before the publishing process began was so encouraging, and I thank you for your honesty and contribution to its growth.

To Mom and Dad, Dr. Romeo and Sarah Escaro, words cannot describe the gratitude that I have for you with supporting me throughout this process. Thank you for believing in me, encouraging me, and being my biggest fans. I am truly blessed to have you as parents and role models and I dedicate this book to you with all of my heart.

To Joe White, Kiera Newnam, and my Get Life Coaching family: There are no coincidences and I truly believe we were brought together for a reason much bigger than ourselves. To Joe, my coach, mentor, teacher, and friend, thank you for the amazing work that you do, your determination to impact the lives of others, and your beautiful, open heart. I am truly blessed to have learned from you, and your guidance has played a significant role in my growth as an individual, allowing my creative voice to be heard. To Kiera, my dear friend and teacher, thank you for your never-ending encouragement, positive outlook, and beautiful spirit that radiates love. I am a lucky girl to have both of you in my life!

To Ernie, my intention for you is unlimited happiness, love, and peace. Thank you for being part of my life's journey and I am sending you so much love and appreciation for the lessons we have learned together.

To the Soul Rocks Books and John Hunt Publishing team,

thank you for all your hard work and dedication to bring my book, starting off as ramblings in my head, to a beautiful piece for the world to enjoy. Special thanks to: my publisher, Alice Grist, for seeing something special with In10tions; Trevor Greenfield, editor; Dominic C. James, copyeditor and proofreader; Nick Welch, cover designer; Stuart Davies, designer; Maria Barry, publicist; Mary Flatt, administration; and Catherine Harris, marketing and public relations.

To John Schulte, thank you for your amazing photography and generosity. You are truly gifted with an amazing talent.

Last but not least, thank you dear reader for taking this journey with me and trusting the process. Wishing you so much love, happiness, and amazing in10tions!

About the Author

Melissa Escaro is a writer and life coach who teaches individuals mind and body connection and personal development skills. She attended the University of Delaware obtaining her Bachelor's degree in Psychology; and Widener University, obtaining her Masters in Clinical Social Work. Her experiences expanded to include mind and body connection through yoga, massage, therapy, Reiki, meditation, and life coaching, focusing on Neuro Linguistic Programming and Ericksonian Hypnotic Language. Melissa's integration of modalities, with her positive outlook, allow her to connect with individuals on many different levels, helping them to make their own connection with their mind and body. She is an active blogger on the Huffington Post and her website: www.melissaekirk.com.

Soul Rocks is a fresh list that takes the search for soul and spirit mainstream. Chick-lit, young adult, cult, fashionable fiction & non-fiction with a fierce twist